|| Shri Prem - Bhuvanbhanu - Jayghosh - Rajendra Chandrashekhar - Jitrakshit Sadgurubhyo Namah ||

THE ULTIMATE QUEST

"Evidences and Logical reasonings for the existence of the soul, rebirth, spirits, karma and supernatural"

Yugpradhaan Aacharya samana Param Pujya Pannyaas Shri Chandrashekhar Vijayji Maharaj Saheb's Disciple Shrutpremi Param Pujya Aacharya Bhagwant Shri Jitrakshitsuriji's Disciple Param Pujya Pannyaas Shri Aaryarakshit Vijayji M.S. Disciple Param Pujya Muni Shri Tatvarshi Vijayji

ISBN 979-8-89446-045-1

AUTHOR'S NOTE

The principles in this book are Universal and Eternal. Universal means they impact across countries, cultures, and religions. Eternal means that they were, they are and they will.

Life without the realization of these principles is just a journey to death. Even if we may or may not realize it, but life moves fast, to avoid regrets towards the end of one's life, one needs to manifest the realization within. A person's life is not measured by its length but by its depth and how well it is spent. Actors make an impression, Great people make an impact.

A book is a capsule of wisdom collected from ages. Acquiring facts is knowledge, Interpreting facts is understanding and the proper application of facts is wisdom. This book will help you gain knowledge and understanding, but wisdom stands for you. Knowledge without action is like plowing without sowing. The objective of education is to bring transformation, not just awareness. Thinking, believing, and knowing what's good is not good enough, but doing is, with its significant goal, life is worth living. If you don't pay the price of living a worthy life, you will have to pay the price of a failed, worthless life. A price has to be paid no matter what. It is better to prepare and prevent, rather than repair and repent.

As the first step, this book focuses on the belief, because to change your reality, it needs first to change your mentality. Every change is not a progress, but every progress is a change.

Read this book and be ready for an amazing journey

'The Ultimate Quest'.

-MUNI TATVARSHI VIJAY

I dedicate this Book to the person who changed my life, My Guiding Star, reverend, Gurudev Pannyaas

Shri Aryarakshit Vijayji M.S

TABLE OF CONTENTS

LET'S START THE

THE ULITIMATE

Quest

FUTURE, The most important thing in the life of every individual. Every person, every creature worries - plans - works- struggles, and aspires to have a better future, a comfortable future. A future that is just filled with happiness, never disturbed by any sort of sorrow. No adversities, only favour of place, person, fate, fame, and power.

Ignorantly or intentionally, every creature strives to secure 'HAPPINESS' for the future. Storing food in ant hills, migration of birds, learning of a kid, earning of a person, investing of an investor, etc. all these examples approve this fact.

Everyone wants to secure happiness: - some find it in survival, some in food, some in home, climate, money, partner, child, power, etc. Everyone has his own way of gaining happiness. 'Source of Happiness' is selected in accordance with how farsighted a person is.

The more a person thinks of his future, the more mature he becomes. MATURITY is the ability to recognize 'What is beneficial and What is not'.

THE FIRST TYPE

Some people, just think about PRESENT. Ignoring or consciously avoiding the upcoming time. Which leads them to commit crimes, be irresponsible, lazy, inconvincible, unfaithful, dishonest, cheat, selfish, etc. They live with a feeling of **"Only present is the Truth, live the life, enjoy the time, who knows tomorrow may be or may not".** Influenced by such thoughts, they actually don't realize how self-centered they have become and how much they are hurting others.

THE SECOND TYPE

Some people have farer vision. They work for achieving their goals which makes them somewhat serious about themselves and brings them some virtues such as hard work, discipline, control of anger, consistency in work, maintaining relations with others in the way they can be helpful ahead, etc. **They are able to do what is right and best rather than what is easy, quick, and convenient.**

Sometimes, it so happens that such people face any problems, cheats, losses, etc. and tangled in the situation they feel that these events have snatched their future.

They try to fight against, start betraying others, telling lies, behaving rude, and implementing every right or wrong way to retrieve the considered source of happiness. But when they fail to regain the loss, they feel that now their future is unsecured, snatched and there are no possibilities to overcome the problem. Being a coward to face the upcoming uncertain future, they decide to end their life, their devastating future and commit suicide.

These victims felt or had an understanding that 'my life is the boundary of my future. Once I end my life I end my future. Ultimately, also ends my worries and I may not have to face anything or anyone. **My life is the truth, if it is finished, I am finished.**

Even if such people do not commit suicide they live a life which is full of misery.

Listen, I am not at all - interested in refuting anyone. My only objective is to keep the truth, the ultimate fact, before you. Perhaps, for sure it may lead everyone to a new vision, to a new way of thinking, decision making, behaving, and understanding, according to Nature = **THE ULTIMATE TRUTH.**

THE THIRD TYPE

On the other hand, there are some people who believe that their present existence, present life, is just a part of their total existence. In their past, they have passed on infinite lives. The current life is just an answer of the previous incarnations and is also the designer, creator, and planner of the upcoming life.

They live the life with an awareness that whatever good happens, is just a return gift of the previous good deeds done at the previous incarnation. Whenever any sorrow or devastating condition befalls in relation to health, fame, business, family, or whatever, they are convinced that these are just the consequences of their own bad deeds done in their previous lives. They believe, "It's my own creation, and selection, which I had agreed to, by committing misdeeds in the past. Now, if I endure the situation without selecting the wrong choices of actions ahead, I can abolish my karma, my debt, over here and free myself by being punished again. The only work which is beneficial to me is to be GOOD.

HENCE, I AM READY TO FACE EVERYTHING. I AM UNSTOPPABLE, UNABLE TO STRESSED BY ANYONE, NO SITUATIONS CAN CONFUSE ME."

These people do not believe in discrimination of skin, gender, religion, creed, race, nation, etc. because they are aware that these things actually don't make the difference, but the growth of qualities, virtues are the only measures which make the difference. It is not the colour or shape of the balloon which decides how high may it fly rather than the gas by which it is filled up.

Friends! This is an awareness, an understanding, a way of living which has amazing benefits. India was a country before, where every citizen was a believer of such beliefs and had gained a glorious past for itself.

For Once, Let's keep aside all these benefits and be somewhat logical, along with a broad mind, open to be convinced by whatever is the truth, with an understanding that:-

**TRUTH IS MINE
RATHER THAN
MINE IS TRUTH.**

All the above beliefs are attached to a core belief. Belief of a thing which, if really exists all the above beliefs become a fact, and if not, it is just a pure fake.

THE CORE BELIEF IS
"EXISTENCE OF SOUL"

The SOUL which is immortal, which travels from life to life, which bonds with karma and faces its results, which never had a start, and never has an end, which is ultimately, similar in every creature but because of karma is expressed differently in every individual.

Is 'SOUL' a scientifically or logically provable fact? Does something like 'SOUL' really Exist in nature?

Here are some of evidences that I would love to share with you. I am confident that this evidences may be helpful to know the most prominent Truth - 'EXISTENCE OF SOUL'.

THE RECOLLECTION OF PAST LIFE MEMORIES

FACT ONE

THE POLLOCK TWINS

On 5th May 1957, while playing on the pavement eleven-year-old Joanna and her six-year-old sister Jacqueline Pollock were run down by a car. When Mrs. Pollock was pregnant later, her husband revealed to her that he had a vision. He saw that she would give birth to twin girls and that these two would be their two lost daughters reborn. Even though Mrs. Pollock was reassured by all gynecologists that there was only one audible heartbeat present and not twins, Mr. Pollock was still convinced that his knowing was correct. Later he proved to be right. On 4th October 1958, Mrs. Pollock gave birth to identical twin girls. The first child was given the name Gillian, the second born ten minutes later was named Jennifer.

While their father was admiring his new daughters, he noticed a scar above the right eyebrow of Jennifer, the younger of the two girls. His recently deceased daughter Jacqueline had the same scar in exactly the same place. She had fallen at the age of three, and a visible scar had remained on her face. To his amazement, he also discovered a brown birthmark the size of his thumb on Jennifer. His deceased daughter Jacqueline had exactly the same birthmark in the same place. All this proved to him that his earlier vision that he had experienced was true. Gillian and Jennifer were truly his first daughters reborn. Mrs. Pollock, being a strict Catholic still rejected the idea of reincarnation until the following events occurred.

When the twins were four months old, the Pollocks moved to a different area. Two-and-a-half years later they returned to visit their old town at Hexam. To the amazement of the parents, their two daughters knew their way around this area extremely well. Without being able to see the school, since it was hidden from sight by the church, one of the girls said, "The school is just around the corner."

The other one pointed to a hill and said, "Our playground was behind there, it had a slide and a swing". When they approached their old house the two sisters recognized it immediately, Even so, Mrs. Pollock unlike her husband, still did not want to believe that the twins were really her recently deceased daughters reborn.

When the twins were four years old, Mr. Pollock opened a box, which had been closed for over three years. In it, he had kept the toys of his first children. He placed some of these outside the twin's bedroom door, as he wanted to see whether they could recognize their toys from the past.

When the girls came out of their room, where their mother stood as witness to their reactions, Jennifer picked up the first doll and said, "Oh! That's Mary (And picking up the second doll) that's my Suzanne! I haven't seen them for ages". She used the same names, which Jacqueline had previously given her two dolls.

"Father Christmas gave us these a long time ago" She turned to Gillian, pointing another toy she said, "And that is your washing machine" Now Mrs. Pollock was finally convinced that her twins really were her first daughters reborn.

THE PERSON WHO CAUGHT HIS MURDERER

In December 1983, a boy named Titu Singh was born in a village near Agra. At the age of four, he began to insist that his name was Suresh Verma and that his wife Uma and his two children lived in Agra and was the owner of a Radio Shop. The entire family was tired of the intense behavior of the boy who insisted on being called Suresh and continually asked to go to Agra. He also talked about having been murdered by two men. He could clearly remember what had happened to him.

One day as he had arrived home in his car and had sounded his horn so that his wife would open the gate, two men came running towards him and shot him in the head. He knew the one who had fired the shot was a businessman called Sedick Johaadien.

During a stay in Agra, Titu's elder brother went to find out whether there really was a Radio Shop with the name his younger brother had mentioned. To his amazement, he found a radio shop with the name 'Suresh Radio Shop'. He went in and asked to see Suresh Verma. He was told that Suresh had been the owner of the shop, But he died several years ago. When he asked for more information about the owner's cause of death, he was advised to go and visit the deceased man's widow Uma Verma.

Uma Verma told him that her husband had been shot in front of their house after returning home in his car. No one knew who had shot him and therefore, the murder had been unsolved.

Titu's brother then informs Uma that his little brother claims to be her deceased husband. He told her everything that Titu had talked about at home. Suresh's widow now insisted on going to see the boy herself.

She also told the rest of her family about this incident, so, Suresh's parents and his three brothers all decided to join her.

When Titu saw his previous parents and his wife he was so happy that he ran up to them and hugged them all. Then he drummed on a stool with his hands to vent his joy just like Suresh used to do when he was a child. A decision was made with his parent's permission to take Titu to Agra to confirm his past life memories.

Once he had arrived there his brothers wanted him to show them the way to the radio shop. They tried to mislead him on purpose, but the four-year-old was not fooled. Even when they told the driver to drive faster as they were approaching the shop, the boy suddenly shouted, "Stop! This is where my shop is".

After the boy had recognized several things from his past, his family was completely convinced that Titu really was their previously murdered son Suresh reborn.

When Professor Chatdah from the University of Delhi heard of the incident he immediately showed great interest in the case. He visited Suresh's widow Uma and asked her what it was that had finally convinced her this boy really was her deceased husband reborn. She said that when she described an incident that only she and her husband knew anything about, Titu was able to remember it clearly. It had been about Suresh having given his wife a big bag of sweets when they were out on a picnic.

Professor Chatdah along with Antonia Mills continued the research. They wanted to clear their doubts regarding the authenticity of this case. All of their research confirmed that they were dealing with an authentic case of reincarnation, Naturally, they also inspected Titu's head to see if he had any scars or birthmarks relating to the shot in the head that had killed him in his previous life, to their amazement they found a dent on the right side of his head which was precisely like the mark of the bullet entering the skull would give. On the other side of his head where the bullet had left the skull in his previous life, they found a star-shaped scar. The wound would naturally have been bigger than the one on the other side of Suresh's head, since a bullet leaving the skull would have made a larger hole than the one entering it.

Titu later even remembered the name of his murderer and when the Agra police questioned the man he confessed to the murder.

Friends!, I would like to inform you that these are not the only couple of cases approving the concept of reincarnation (rebirth) by the people recollecting past life memories. But, There are really a vast number of cases all around the world. The above-mentioned cases are just samples. If you wish you can study even some other amazing authentic and recently occurred cases by having a Google search:-

1) Imad Elawar (reincarnation case) 

2) Munesh Bhajan Singh reincarnation case 

3) Joan grant reincarnation 

4) Shanti Devi (reincarnation case) 

5) Ismail Altinkilic and Cevriye Bayri (reincarnation cases) 

Even there are books written on this subject a few of them are :

1) Where Reincarnation and Biology Intersect - Ian Stevenson, M.D.

2) Children's past lives - Carol Bowman

3) Lifetimes – True accounts of reincarnation – Frederick Lenz

4) Life before Birth – Peter and Mary Harrison

5) You will live again – Brad Steiger

Logic One

We remember our own childhood even when we are grown up. Because we were the ones who had actually experienced our own childhood. In the same way, there are some people who can even recollect their own past life. Because they were the ones who had actually experienced those past lives.

Friends!, I assume that you may have a question 'Why only those some people can remember their past life and not me / everyone? Are they Lucky? - Oh Dear!, you may not know, But really you are the luckiest as you are reading this book. I am sure that you may get a very satisfying answer as you read ahead and... and ...also my next book

" Origin of The Original".

I may like to ask you, which is that thing, that stuff, which connected the memories, the feelings, between Joanna and Gillian, Jacqueline and Jennifer, Suresh and Titu.

The previous body was burned to ashes or buried beneath the earth along with the brain, heart, nervous system, etc. Every part, every system, of the body, faced the same end.

Not any cell, tissue, gene, DNA, nerve, or vein was carried forward in the new body even then, how did the above fact come true? What was similar to both the bodies due to which the transmission of personality took place?

The answer is: - "Soul".

Now let's see some true incidents of persons living in spirit after death proving, in addition, the second Truth,

The second fact that is..... Read ahead.

FACT TWO

EXISTENCE OF GHOST

THE CHAIR OF *Death*

In 1702, there was a Tavern, located near Sandhutton in North Yorkshire, England. Thomas Busby, a notorious gangster used to come there to have drinks and enjoy the pub, on his favourite chair. Busby was so fond of his chair that he could never bear anyone else sitting on it. If someone dared to sit on it, he made such a fuss that he disturbed the staff and even other customers. Busby had such awe that they had to keep the chair empty.

One night, Busby came to the Pub with his father-in-law, Daniel Auty, and he drank heavily. They had an argument about Busby's wife, Auty's daughter Elizabeth. Then for some reason, Busby went out of the bar. When he returned, he found Daniel sitting on his chair. He ordered him to vacate but Daniel didn't respond anyway. They had a dispute and the controversy escalated. Busby, intoxicated through alcohol, killed his father-in-law and also killed those who intervened to free them.

Within a few minutes, the police came and arrested Busby. He was sentenced to death. When he was asked for his last request, he desired a drink of ale on his favorite chair. Before being hung he declared, "Listen everyone! the bar chair is only made for me. No one else is allowed to sit on it. If someone may dare, then this Busby will come from the world beyond and kill those persons." He was convicted in 1702.

The bar owner was happy with the idea that the terror would stop after Busby's death. Now there was no need to leave Busby's chair empty.

As soon as he went to the chair, he started feeling strange. He felt that Busby's soul was wandering around that chair. Realizing that this might be a superstition of his own mind, he ignored the feeling and continued his work. Suddenly there were words in his ear "This chair is just for me .....If ...... someone sits on it ..., I will not let him live……, I will kill him…. I will kill him….." the voice seemed familiar, it was the voice of Busby, the bar-owner panicked. He sold it to a man named Ernasho. However, he didn't even hide the fact Ernasho and sat on the chair. They were soldiers and lived in a disciplined way. So, they drank the right amount, and later on, while returning back, not even two miles away, their car crashed and both of them lost their lives. The next day, Ernasho read the news with photos of two Air Force soldiers killed in a car accident. He was convinced that the cause of their death was nothing else than the chair. He felt sad for them.

A few days later, an Army Major came to the bar to have a drink. The whole bar was packed. Only that chair was empty. He got there and read the instructions placed on the chair. Seeing him, Ernasho also came over there. He explained the whole fact and persuaded him not to sit on that chair.

But the Major laughed at him and called his thoughts superstitious "I want to sit on this chair" He told the bar owner. "Let's see what happens to me! Listen! let's have a bet. If I come back here safely after six months, I will win and if I don't, you will win and keep the amount of bet." Ernasho replied, "I don't want to make such a bet, but my inner voice says that you must not sit." Ignoring his warnings, the Major sat down and took his drink, waving a victory sign on his face.

Meanwhile, he began to feel as if something strange was happening to his body. Within two to three days he realized that he was suffering from some unknown disease. Doctors were not able to diagnose his disease. It worsened and he was in great pain.

However, he said that whenever he used to be in a state of semi-consciousness he saw that empty chair of Ernasho's bar and heard someone threatening him, "This chair is mine, why you dared to sit over there! You were warned foolish! Let's have fun now". When Ernasho heard about the tragedy from other army officer, he became convinced that the Major's untimely death was due to an empty chair lying in front of his eyes.

The Death Chair has "killed" every person who sat on it, no matter who and how. Eventually, the pub owner moved it into the basement hoping that nobody would sit in it. However, one day a delivery man sat on it. An hour later he crashed his truck and died, after his death, the landlord asked the local museum to take it. To ensure nobody sat in it again, they hung the chair seven feet high from the ground. The person who sat in the chair experiences haunting experiences including extreme itching, paranoia, hearing things, confusion, items being moved and written warnings on mirrors and walls about the person's imminent murder in addition to many other strange happenings. At present the chair is preserved at the Thirsk museum.

THE DEAD STILL ON DUTY

Captain Harbhajan Singh was a soldier of the 23rd Battalion of the Punjab Regiment. He died in 1968 while patrolling the INDO - CHINA border at Nathula in Sikkim.

He was slightly behind his comrades and was suddenly struck by ice and died. Fellow soldiers did not know what happened to him and where he was. They looked around but found no clue of him. One day four to six soldiers had a dream. In it, Harbhajan Singh appeared and said, "I have found my dead body lying under the snow in some place take it out and complete my funeral ceremonies." They started exploring the place described in the dream. After much hard work, Harbhajan Singh was found dead under a heap of snow. He was taken out and cremated.

Harbhajan Singh was 26 years old when he died. After his death, his soul was constantly present on his duty.

His soul was seen patrolling the border even when the peaks of Sikkim were covered with snow due to heavy snowfall. So, the soldiers often saw him as a deity. He was seen patrolling with the same uniform he was wearing on the day of his death and with a gun in his hand. Even Chinese soldiers also apprised their officers that in such freezing cold, an armed Indian soldier is always seen standing on the border without wearing a single warm blanket or garments.

Harbhajan's soul assured his superiors that they would not worry about the protection of the border. He will always protect it. And if there may be some possibility of any trouble he will give three days advance notice. It really happened. This made the officers confident about security. They all felt and felt that Harbhajan Singh was present there and many times he even became visible.

The Indian army had set up a separate barrack and office for Harbhajan. A chair was also placed for him during the flag meetings between the Indian army and the Chinese army. Harbhajan used to come and sit there as a deity.

All facilities were given to Harbhajan Singh as a living soldier despite from the fact that he is actually dead. He was also given two months leave in a year. Arrangements were also made for him to go home during the holidays. Seats were reserved by his name in Siliguri Express (Dibrugarh Express). Shortly before the trip, a fellow soldier would place his luggage under the berth and make a bed on it. His uniform was also placed on the berth. This fellow soldier would sit on the berth next to him and take care of him so that no one would sit in his place or take away those things. When they came to Jalandhar station, he was taken out of the vehicle with his bed, uniform, etc. and from there he was taken by a jeep to Kuke village in Punjab's Kapurthala district where he would visit his parents. He was also given a promotion considering his noble performance. For 30 years after his death, he voluntarily worked as a GHOST in border security.

Then he expressed his desire for retirement to the Army officers, They had to accept it. He eventually retired with all the great honors that a living soldier deserves. Before Harbhajan Singh retired, a temple was also built in Nathula Sikkim in his memory which later was visited by many people. His puja aarti is also performed there. It is said that there are many occasions when his soul proves his presence over there. In the temple, there is a room to live in and also a resting room. At night the sheets are fairly clean and wrinkle-free in bed but when viewed in the morning they look chaotic, a little messy, and wrinkled. It clearly looks like someone had used the bed, his polished boots are muddy and covered with dust or snow.

To know more about Non-frictional Ghost cases Search :-

(1) Spirit of grey lady Dame Sybil Penn 

(2) Spirit of Flight Engineer Don Repo and Bob loft 

(3) Rosemary Brown Spirit connections 

(4) Arthur Stilwell Spirit connections 

(5) Mystery Appearance of Sri Yantra Geoglyph in Oregon Dry Lake Bed 

Even there are some books:-
(1) Haunted Royal Homes - Joan Forman
(2) 30 Years Among the Dead - Carl Wickland
(3) The Ghost Whisperer - Katie Coutts
(4) Ghost Watch - Colin Gardner
(5) Understanding Ghosts - Victoria Branden, Victor Gollancz
(6) Ghost Sightings - Collin Wilson

Logic Two

Which is that thing which continued to express the presence of the person who had already died? The dead person was buried or burnt away, along with even the brain, heart, etc. was also given an end. Even so, how does that ghost know every detail of the deceased and insist on being known as the person who is no more?

If we don't believe in the existence of the soul how the above fact did came true?

Friends!, here we have no other option rather accepting the existence of the soul. The above incident even drives us to an additional fact which is also proven i.e. the soul can transform its way of existence from human to ghost[1](dev) and if it is possible to be a ghost from human why we can't be an animal, insect, plant, bird, etc. Even they are living creatures and life is not possible without the presence of the soul.

So, the SECOND FACT is '**It is possible to change The Way of Existence**'. Even if we are born as a human in the present life, in our upcoming life, we can be each and every creation of life that exist around us.

We can even be a human of any country, race, creed, religion, or gender; we can even be an animal like a lion, tiger, giraffe, rhino, dog, cat, pig, rat, etc; we can even be a fish like a whale, dolphin, shark, octopus, etc... we can even be an insect like a bee, housefly, caterpillar, lizard, cockroach, mosquito, etc. we can be a vegetation like a tree, shrub, herb, flower, cactus, plant, fruit, seed, nut etc. All of these, including a large list of subspecies within their type, these all can be our possible next life, next birth, and the next role to be played. Someone's present can be our imminent future.

Friends! Do you want to know on which basis our future is decided. **Let's see the 3rd evidence I am sure that it would help us to understand the secrets of our upcoming lives.**

[1]It's important to be clear that Ghosts are not at all wandering bodyless souls. They have body, but of a different type than the body of us. Due to which they are able to be visible or invisible, change their appearance, etc. Even they breathe, consume food, and face birth and death.

PAST LIFE REGRESSION THERAPY

FACT THREE

In the content of this part major References are taken from
'The Karma Hand Book' - Trutz Hardo

SHORT INTRODUCTION TO PAST LIFE REGRESSION THERAPY (PLR THERAPY)

Past life regression therapy is a Hypnotic therapy by which a person is made able to access the subconscious mind and recollect past life memories.

In order to access this information person is made to go into the so-called "Alpha-state", a stage of consciousness attained between the waking-the Beta state and the sleeping state. In the Alpha state, the analytical controlling left hemisphere is turned off and the right hemisphere of the brain containing the subconscious is turned on as much as possible and that leads to the past life. To understand the therapy properly, Let us observe the therapist talk:-

"Before accepting appointments on the phone or in a pre-talk we attempt to establish whether such a treatment is possible for the client whether immediately or at a later time. The only restriction is for those already under psychiatric care or treatment, in which case the permission of the current therapist or medical doctor is required to avoid disturbing a treatment already in progress.

A complete anamnesis is carried out, so the therapist can get a very clear picture not only of the symptoms of the particular problem to be treated but also of the total life situation e.g.- life history, family, occupation, general status of present or past illnesses of the client. Then we explain to the client how the therapy will be carried out. If the decision has been made by both client and therapist to begin immediately with the therapy, the client is asked to lie or sit in a comfortable position.

As soon as the client has been put in the alpha state he is led in his imagination over a meadow to a healing source where he is asked to feel the healing power of the water while drinking and later, after his return from his earlier lives he will take a healing bath in this source.

Finally, we have him imagine a bed of clouds in which he is asked to lie down and to feel himself clothed and protected by divine energy. At this point, he meets his generally invisible higher self. The higher self knows everything about the client even about his earlier lives for it represents his own higher knowledge the direct contact between him and the divine sphere.

The client asks the higher self to lead him to the source of the problem or symptom.

The higher self takes his hand leading him to one of many gates in a long wall of clouds behind which he finds his parents or one of his past lives. Here the theme of the present sitting or "session" is precisely formulated and it is also determined that the client upon a count of three will find himself in the life related to the question. It will be exactly one day previous to the beginning of an event important for the development of his present symptoms or problem. In most cases, we will find that they are in a life as victims. The client then discovers who and where he is, what his name is, what country he is in, if he is married or single, what his profession is etc.

Then he is led to the event of the following day. Here he experiences the causes of his present problem or symptoms. This re-experiencing is not the same as in reality, but as in a mental form, i.e. tears may run but seldom is pain actually felt. After that, brought again before the wall of clouds, the client learns from the higher self that some participants in his just re-experienced life have also re-appeared in his present life (Souls from the different bodies throughout many lives meet again and again until they have found harmony among themselves). Afterward, the higher self is asked if there still is one or more earlier lives in which other causes for the present symptoms may be found. If the answer is 'yes' the process begins once more and the search begins again for a life as a victim of another life of suffering and retribution.

If all the necessary causes have been found in lives as a victim and re-experienced usually in an emotional way then the higher self will be asked before the gate of clouds to now take the client to the life or lives where the actual cause of suffering can be found. The higher self then leads the client in a previous so-called "life as a perpetrator", in which he has caused other persons suffering or pain. Here the actual primary cause is found for the symptom or problem later manifesting itself in lives as a victim and still felt as a symptom or problem in his present one.

In such life as a perpetrator, the soul has carried out an action making it not only guilty for others but also in its own eyes. This feeling of guilt often remains present in the subconscious over many lives and can develop into a guilty complex of unknown origin leading to depression, inferiority complexes, and helper syndromes. Therefore it is very important also to experience life as a perpetrator to free the person permanently from his guilty feelings during the dissolution process. This will also help him to forgive more easily those who have caused him pain and suffering during his life as a victim. Now he may understand that there is a higher meaning and a just purpose, nothing happens in accordance with the law of karma that the person has not caused himself.

After re-experiencing all the relevant earlier lives chosen by the higher self, the client is led to the so-called mountain of revelation from this higher vantage - point the earlier lives spread out before him can be compared with his present life. Also recognizing their interconnection with his present life.

After that, the higher self gives him a Golden Cup like a golden chalice with a liquid containing the power of Love, Forgiveness, and Dissolution of suffering and guilt. The client takes this cup into his life as a perpetrator and asks forgiveness to all those who have suffered because of him. Then he offers the cup to the perpetrator who he was himself, thus releasing himself from all guilt.

After that, he takes the cup into each of the lives where he himself was as a victim discovered in the sessions and starts forgiving all of those who have brought him suffering and pain. Finally, offering the cup to the person he himself was and thus freeing his earlier self from all suffering and pain over there. He then takes the cup into his present life, where he offers it to everyone whom he now knows to have been either a victim or perpetrator in one of his earlier lives. Forgiving them or asking them for forgiveness for his former or present offenses against them. Finally, he stands in front of himself and forgives himself for all the evils done by him to others in earlier lives or in the present one.

As the next step, the higher self gives him a large open Pinecone. Into whose spaces, he now stuffs everything he would like to give up including his feelings of guilt. The filled cone is then burned with all its contents in a bright fire and all stuffed-in items are returned to the original source of all Love. Then the client formulates his resolution affirmation beginning as follows: "I am free of !. . " after this affirmation is repeated several times, he is led back to the bed of clouds and finally back to the healing source to take the healing bath and from there back into the here and now in the present situation.

SEARCH FOR GRACE

In 1987, Dr. Bruce Goldberg received a phone call from a woman in her thirties named Ivy. She explained that she had twice seen him on television. This encouraged her to pick up the phone and arrange an appointment for Regression therapy.

When she came to his Clinic in Baltimore, she gave him the impression of being polite and rather shy. Her reason for coming to see him was to find out why she had such a destructive relationship with her friend John who abuses her physically and psychologically and had almost killed her three times. John was insincere, unpredictable, and egoistic. Nonetheless she could not let him go. She was quick to forgive his behaviour and his brutality after he promised her each time that it would never happen again.

At the same time, Ivy felt drawn to another man Dave who seemed to be the total opposite of John. He was polite, loving, trustworthy, and had not much experience with women.

Ivy's dilemma was that she was fond of both men; valuing Dave's sincere and deep love and yet not being able to give up her passionate addiction to John. Everything pointed toward a decision in favour of Dave, but still, she could not let go of John. On top of all these, she was plagued by nightmares in which a man repeatedly murdered her. She had the feeling that it was John even though he looked completely different and wore a different clothes. She suffered from sleeplessness, since after nightmares it was difficult to go back to sleep. She then feared going to sleep, afraid that she would be subjected to more disturbing dreams.

During regression, she suddenly saw herself back in the year 1925. Her name was Grace Doze and was 31 years old. She was having an argument with Chester, her husband. He was an employee of General Electric. They had a one-year-old son by the name of Cliff. He often stayed with Grace's Mother in the same village. Her husband accused her of having affairs with other men. When Dr. Goldberg asked her whether this was true, she admitted it was and said that her idiot husband did not know how to make her happy. She was in the prime of her life, attractive, and could not envisage herself being faithful. Sometimes they fought with each other, but she felt strong enough to cope with him.

The following year they both moved into a flat in the main street of Buffalo. She continued to find her husband Chester boring and went out alone in the evenings and hitched rides in cars to get to her destinations. She found being picked up exciting since she could get to know interesting men this way. She had a friend called Mary who attended wild parties with her. When asked about the next important event in her life, Grace described a heated dispute with her husband on the 19th of April 1927 during which she injured his arm with a pair of scissors.

Next, she saw herself two weeks later with a man called Jack. He appeared to have fallen in love with her and reassured her that he wished to stay in Buffalo in order to be with her. He seemed to like everything about Grace. She now decided to leave her husband and rent a room in a hotel. In contrast to her relationship with her husband, she never fought with Jack even though he showed signs of having a jealous streak. On the 17th of May, Chester tried to persuade her to come back to him after he had found her in the hotel. She managed to escape from him and Jack drove her to another hotel to rent another room. After that, Jack took her to a swimming pool, where she usually swam every week. He had been out drinking. Later, Jack picked Grace up from there. In the car, He suggested that they should move somewhere else. Grace told him that she would definitely want to take her son with her. He was very indignant about this. Then he got cross with her, saying that the man in the pub told him that she was a whore. He also made nasty remarks about her clothes and her shoes with the red heels. The man at the reception had told him exactly whom she had slept with. She strongly contradicted him and accused him of being drunk. He called her a tart. He suddenly stopped the car, hit her, stabbed her with a knife and finally strangled her.

After death, we are usually able to see everything from a bird's perspective without feeling any more pain. Goldberg led Ivy into this state of being immediately after death. He allowed her to describe through the eyes of Grace what happened to her at that time. Jack had thrown her body into the Ellicott creek. When asked who Jack was in her present life, she named her earlier friend John whom she had traded in for Dave. When asked whether Chester or her son Cliff had been reborn in her present life, she replied that they had not.

Such dramatic murder stories and other powerful occurrences from past lives are often revealed during regression therapy. Dr. Goldberg gave no great personal significance to Ivy's account since it had been accessed in a trance state. He did not consider it his duty to double-check the material obtained during regression for its true content. "I don't concern myself with names, dates, or places since these have no therapeutic value". Therefore, this case was added to his files.

Three years later, he happened to go through these notes and noticed that Ivy had used her full name which was Grace Doze and the place where she had lived in Buffalo, New York. She also named the day of her death as the 17th May 1927. Only now he had the idea to write to a newspaper in Buffalo to inquire whether it existed in 1927, and during the third week of May there had been a news report about the murder of a woman named Mrs. Grace Doze. Neither Dr. Goldberg nor Ivy had ever been to Buffalo.

Even Dr. Goldberg was surprised by what came to light. Three Buffalo-based newspapers reported various issues about a mysterious murder that was not solved. Dr. Goldberg was then sent copies of these papers which had been preserved on microfilm. In these papers were reports of the discovery of the body of Mrs. Grace Doze who was found in the Ellicott creek. According to the medical autopsy report, knife wounds were found on her body as well as strangulation marks on her neck. She wore shoes with red heels. Daily the newspapers announced more details about this murder case.

All the names mentioned were accurate except two that Ivy had talked about during hypnosis. All the details such as her surname, husband's name, mother's surname, street name, names of hotels in which she had stayed, her visit to the swimming pool, her friend's name, various incidents in her personal life as well as the disputes with her husband were confirmed. The police had questioned her husband and held him temporarily as a possible murder suspect. Everything was completely accurate. The papers did report that Graze Doze had been 30 years old when she died and that her son was called Chester like his father, only these two were the exceptions.

Dr. Goldberg told many people from Television companies about this fascinating case. C.B.S television was the company that finally decided to make a film out of these events using famous actors. The Personal History of Grace was thoroughly researched during the making of this Film. From this, they were able to discover her correct age which was just as Ivy had stated and contrary to what the newspaper wrote. Another discovery was that her son was not called Chester as the papers had wrongly reported but the name was Clifford shortened to Cliff just as Ivy had mentioned while speaking as Grace. During regression even if Ivy had tried to deceive Dr. Goldberg by having read newspaper articles from the past and had informed herself about Grace Doze, she would have given him the wrong details. Her success during regression was only possible because she was able to spontaneously let herself go into a deep trance state. In such a trance, one can no longer play roles or tell lies since what is revealed is the actual past life experience.

The film 'Search for Grace' was broadcast by C.B.S. on the 17th May 1994 at 11 pm. This film was shown exactly 67 years to the day after the death of Grace Doze and at the exact time of her death.

Friends! Regression Therapy is a medical stream, a way to cure the patients. There are a number of therapists around the world able to access the past life/lives. Hence, to explain the authenticity of PLR therapy; I am over here with just a single example. As you can even have the PLR and explore your own past life. The further examples are focused on introducing the third truth.

RELEASE OF THE *Disease*

Robert is forty-four years old. He is allergic to pollen, especially birch pollen and various grasses. From April to June a swollen and constantly runny nose tortures him. Tears flowing from his eyes, coughing and above all those, difficulties in breathing. A day before the planned session he called up to ask for an urgent emergency treatment for his terrible breathing difficulties. After putting him into the alpha state his present life was investigated for possible causes. At the age of three, he experienced his first traumatic loss of breath on a picnic excursion. After eating, his parents took a nap in the rather high grass while he ran around playing. Suddenly he fell down with his nose directly on a dandelion flower whose seeds flew and landed in his nose.

(Robert coughed violently at this point in the session)

At the age of ten, smoke from a Bengal light got in his nose. He suddenly could no longer breathe and was also made fun of by various bystanders. At the age of sixteen a teacher hit him on the chest during Boxing training, causing him to lose his breath and fall almost unconscious to the floor. In the Army, they trained him by making him run with the gas masks on. He could not breathe and saved himself from suffocation by sticking a finger between his gas mask and his face to let the air in. These similar occurrences were, as we would discover later all only karmic repercussions of earlier events.

Upon being asked, his higher self led him into a life in medieval Russia. He saw himself as a Knight armed with a spear and a bludgeon, who was just in the process of attacking a Castle along with other knights.

They succeeded in over running the Castle but in the courtyard of the Castle, burning tar was thrown on him and he was hit in the chest by a spear. Despite the pain, Robert perceived the stinking smell of his burning leather suit and the feeling of his burning skin (Robert began again to cough violently) while still trying to pull the spear out of his chest. He fell to the ground and died.

In his next life, he is a twelve-year-old boy. He has to dive together with other boys for pearls. A man finds enjoyment in pushing him underwater to show how strong he is. But the boy panics and his lungs fill with water.

In another life, he is a Russian soldier named Egon who fought in 1792 against the French. While pushing a canon, he slips and falls into the mud where one of the cannon's wheels rolls over his chest. During the attack no one can care for him, so he lies for there about 15 minutes before dying.

In a still earlier life, he is a five-year-old boy to whom his tribe has just sacrificed by throwing him into the sea to soothe the wrath of the water god.

His higher self shows him now his life as a perpetrator as the causal life, as the life which becomes the 'cause' for the many upcoming lives of karmic suffering.

In one life far back in time, he was a sorcerer who carried out human sacrifices by killing his victims with smoke and incantations. In later life, he belonged to a group of henchmen responsible for capturing and imprisoning women declared to be witches.

His "specialty" was putting a sack over the head of the captured women allowing them hardly enough air to breathe. After their conviction, they were generally burnt at the stake. One of these women is his present wife.

After Robert had gone into all these earlier lives with the Golden Cup and had carried out the ritual of forgiving and being forgiven, he returned to the beta state and opened his eyes. His nose was suddenly completely free of congestion and his coughing attacks had completely disappeared. He exclaimed joyfully, "All my problems have disappeared".

The karmic retribution for his two earlier lives as a perpetrator had lasted many lives even down to the present one. Having recognized the reasons for his former hard-heartedness, by the act of retribution his karmic balancing process was now complete. This is a phenomenon demonstrated again and again by regression therapy.

ARROW OF

Eberhard was facing problems such as depression inferiority complex fears, allergies, heart-muscle disturbance (five months in the hospital) headaches, migraines (with vomiting), feeling of tightness, bronchitis, asthma, fear of people, fear of being disappointed, claustrophobia (he cannot enter elevators), hemophilia, neck and back problems, tinnitus and dizziness, his chin is often out of joints he had a number of problems with his mother, etc...etc...etc.

In a supervision seminar on Past life regression, Four diploma candidates were selected to discover and eliminate (with occasional interventions by the instructor) the reason for Eberhard's tinnitus which had suddenly begun a year earlier.

The tinnitus was constantly present in the left ear, must worse than in the right one. He already had an ear infection as a child. For the sake of simplicity, let us begin with his life as a perpetrator.

Eberhard recognizes himself as Heinrich, the master of a German castle. He is fifty-one years old but he had no children with his wife Katharina. There is a war, as another castle lord wants to take possession of his land. Henrich's soldiers have taken numerous prisoners. They are tied up and stretched to the wall and unpleasant liquids are poured with a funnel into their mouths.

Heinrich enjoys these tortures and is watching with satisfaction. At his own pleasure, he also takes part in the torturing. **He takes a bow and arrow and shoots a tied man in his left ear to see how deep the arrow will go.** The prisoner cries in anguish but dies very soon from the wound.

The callous Heinrich gives up his body at the age of seventy-four. His list of sins is outrageous.

Four of the karmic resolving earlier lives connected to his present tinnitus were investigated. In The Brazilian jungle, he is a man named Joni. He is a hunter armed with a bow and arrow and despite his thirty-five years of age he is still unmarried, he loves being alone. On the day of his death, a cut-down tree falls on his neck jabbing a branch into his left ear. He dies immediately lying on his stomach.

In one of his next lives, he is an Eskimo woman named Kiri, forty-four years old with three children and an alcoholic husband, who beats his wife and children. Once again he is about to start beating his children but Kiri, their mother, tries to protect them. He throws her head first against the wall. Her head suddenly starts to buzz, and nausea overcomes her. She is dizzy, and the pain in her neck starts to spread into her head. Suddenly she cannot hear any longer, she sees the children crying and lies down on the floor. She can only see the mouth movements of her angry husband, but cannot understand what he was saying.

She is led to the day before her death. She is now sixty-two years old and still living with her husband, whom she hates. The childrens have left. Since the day of that incident she is deaf, so they can only communicate by hand signs. The back of her head still hurts, and she often has dizzy spells and headaches.

In another life, Ebarhard is a forty-eight-year-old man in Tunisia. His name is Amir. He wears a turban and trades in camels. Amir falls off a camel and while falling, is hit by its hoof on his left ear and jaw. His left jawbone is broken. Although he is treated, the jaw never heals. He died at the age of sixty-seven from heart and breathing problems.

And there was another life as a victim, a Karmic cause for the problems with his left ear. In 1920 he was Jean, the owner of a Paris nightclub, who always kept 6-8 girls ready for his masculine customers. He was unmarried but slept with his prostitutes. At the same time, he was corrupt - and stingy, for which he was hated. When he was fifty-three, two men with pistol broke into his beautiful house, tied him up and hit on the left cheek and ear with the butt of their guns to make him open the safe. After they had cleaned out the safe, One of them pointed his pistol at him, says, "You dirty pig!" and

pulls the trigger. The bullet hit him directly below his left ear. He died immediately. His "never-again" sentence was formulated
 As follows: "I will never again cheat others. I will never again abuse women or degrade them sexually. I will never again misuse my power or be attached to wealth".

On the Mountain of Revelation, Eberhard recognizes the causal effect of the law of Karma and accepts it as just. After he has given the cup of forgiveness to all the others mistreated by Heinrich in his callousness and criminal brutality and asked for their forgiveness, he carries the Golden Cup to his soul as Heinrich, forgiving him too for what he has done... Then he goes into his life as a victim and forgives all those who caused him suffering. This all was easier for him now because he knows that he himself had chosen the pain, for instance, the brutal husband of Kiri in order to attain Karmic retribution through his mistreatment as the cause of her deafness.

To know more about the PLR therapy and other amazing cases you can read:-

1	**2**	**3**
The Search for Bride Murfy **– Morey Bernstein**	**Many Lives, Many Masters** **– Dr. Brian Weiss**	**Past Lives, Future Lives** **– Dr. Bruce Goldberg**

4	**5**
Life before Life **– Helen Wambach**	**Journey Of Souls** **– Michael Newton Phd.**

Logic Three

Here, we can simply understand how the existence of the Soul is proven. So now let's discuss the additional fact.

We had seen in the case of Robert, that he had breathing problems only because in his previous life as henchman or sorcerer he harassed others and committed such deeds. Eberhard had his tinnitus only because in the life as Heinrich he had used that arrow to measure how deep it may insert in the ear. Here we can see clearly that mistake of a single life can have its retribution till many upcoming lives. Those and many other somewhat similar examples (which I have not mentioned here. But are written in books or recorded as Case History Files by PLR Therapist) derive the Third Truth, **THE ULTIMATE JUDGE OF NATURE.**

Every action has a reaction. We have to pay for our way, Nothing happens by chance, There is no injustice for anyone, No crimes are hidden, Every mistake has a punishment, and we get what we give..... That's the "KARMA".

Our upcoming life is developed by our own deeds, our own karma. Till the time we were unaware of this concept, this Fact, this law of Nature – "Karma" we kept on deciding our upcoming lives unknowingly under the charge of previous karma. But, now as we know the Karma we don't need to continue this blind game ahead. Every punishment we face and endure in our life is the fruit, the result of "Karma" (bad deeds) and Every Gift we receive in our life is the result of "Dharma" (good deeds).

In the logical part of the 1st Fact, a question arose which I said to be answered later, let's remember that question:-

"Why only those some people can remember their past life and not me / everyone? Are they Lucky?" Here is the solution to the first question – Every one of us through PLR therapy can not only remember the past life but also know the karmic cause of the various situations we face in our present life. So, not only those some lucky people only can know their past life but **even we and everyone can know about it.** Here, we have completed the first question now let's start the second,

"Are they Lucky?" The answer is "Yes" They are. Here we are able to recognize two types of situations 1) persons remembering their past life on their own. 2) By Regression Therapy. As the concept of karma is proven now, it will help us to understand why such difference takes place. According to "The Complete" (**To know this Mr. Complete you must have to read my next Book "ORIGIN OF THE ORIGINAL".)** The one who conducts the rituals given below can recollect his past life memories in the next life.

ब्रह्मचर्येण तपसा सद्धैदाध्ययनेन च।
विद्यामन्त्रविशेषेण सत्तीर्थासेवनेन च।।
पित्रोः सम्यगुपस्थानाद् ग्लानभैषज्यदानतः।
देवादिशोधनाच्चैव भवेज्जातिस्मरः पुमान्।।

If you are able to understand the above verses you have got the answer, and if not, let me give a clue, a direction to understand the above verses.

The Clue is: - Get, Approach a Guru, but not a linguistic expert and under his presence, his aura and blessings know not only the meanings but also the mysteries hidden in these verses.

Now let's switch to the next evidence.

FACT FOUR

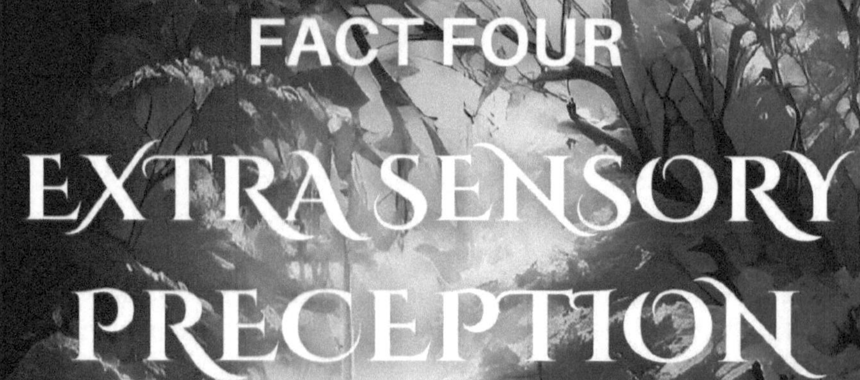

EXTRA SENSORY PRECEPTION

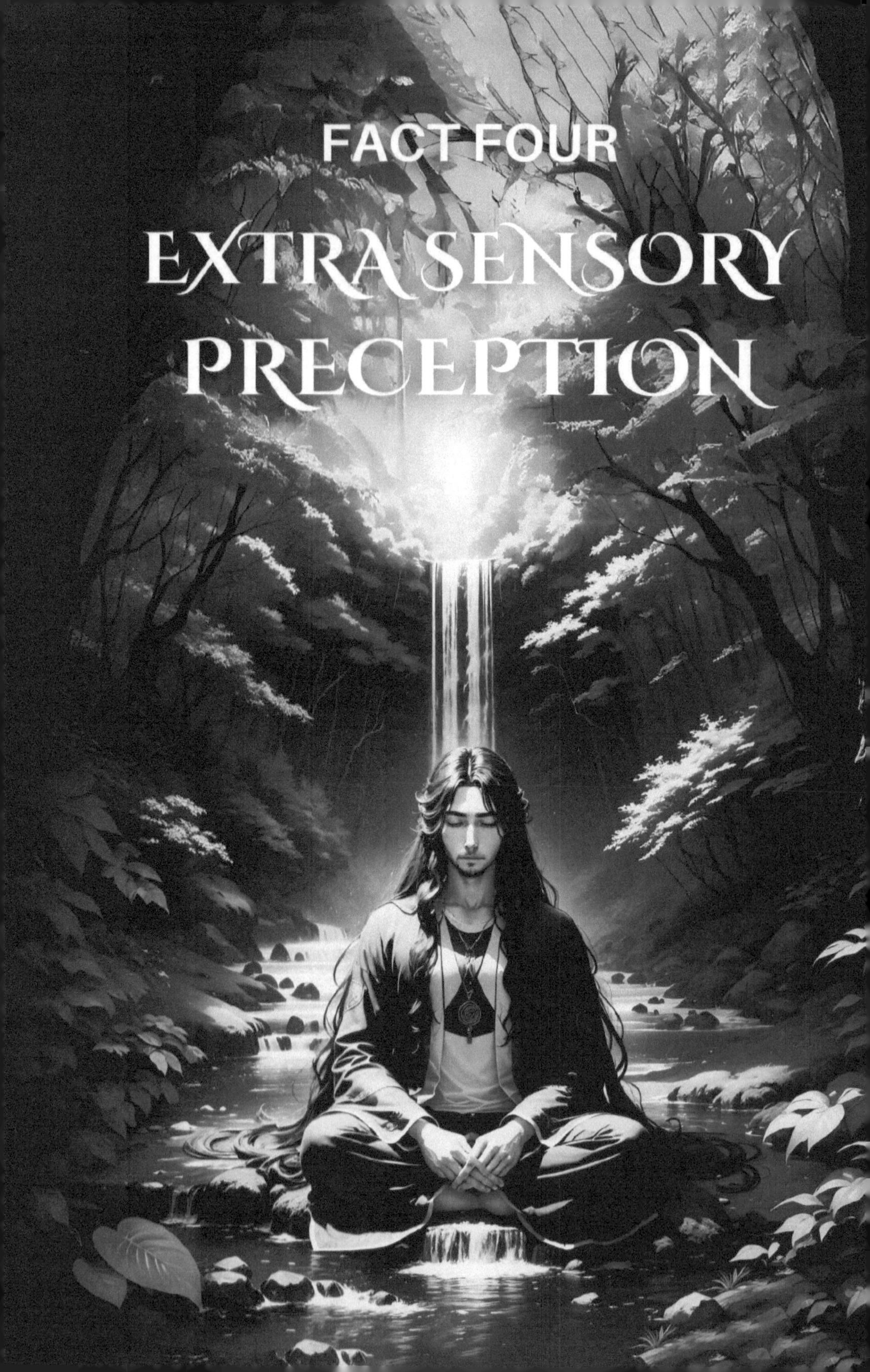

JIM THE WONDER DOG

Marshall, Missouri was the hometown of Jim, the Wonder Dog. Jim was an English Llewellin setter with remarkable abilities as demonstrated via the instruction of his owner Sam Arsdale. Sam originally just wanted a hunting dog, but he got a lot more than he bargained for.

Jim's master realized Jim's power when Jim was four years old. Once, Sam was sitting in the hotel's garden and he told Jim to go and sit under a tree. Jim immediately ran there and sat down. A few moments later, Sam told him to go and stand under another tree and he went and stood under the same tree. Sam was surprised by this ability for as many trees or shrubs name Sam said, Jim identified them all.

Sam then learns that Jim can recognize even different vehicles. When he mentioned the names of ten different vehicles, Jim approached them and identified them by putting his paw on them. Moreover, even if he listened to the license number of the car, he was able to identify the car relating to that number.

Then Sam realizes that Jim also has the power to know what's going to happen in the future. Sam once asked his Dog, "Which horse will win in the race that starts soon?" Jim came near a horse and pointed at him by touching his paw to the horse. A few minutes later the race started and the same horse that Jim had shown won the race.

Then Sam did another experiment. He collected the names of the horses that took part in the second race and wrote their different names on different papers. Then Sam asked Jim "Which of the named horses will win in the next race?" Not once, but each time whichever horse's name had been indicated by Jim, the same horse won the race. Sam had asked these questions in the presence of many people. Sam himself was not a gambler. So he never tried to win a prize in the horse race with the help of his dog. Moreover, he also made sure that no gambler's reward was tarnished by the power of his dog.

The fact that Sam had no passion for making money from his beloved Dog can also be evident by another incident. Once, he refused an offer from a well-known filmmaker to show off Jim's strengths and earn millions of dollars in compensation. However, he gave the necessary consent to the scientists who wanted to do research on his dog with psychic powers. From 1929 to 1933 teams of different scientists tested the Dog's power, including Prof. Durant & Prof. Dikson from the University of Missouri. This team of scientists organized a public experiment in Colombia with the presence of about 900 people. Scientists instructed Jim in different languages such as Spanish, Italian and German. Jim followed their instructions without making the slightest mistake. Naturally, the dog was not familiar with all these languages. During the experiment, a scientist instructed him in Spanish to find a woman dressed in blue and wearing a white hat. Jim took a look at the people sitting there and immediately he ran to a woman, exactly according to the instructions wearing a blue suit and a white hat and put his toes on her feet. Another scientist instructed Jim in Italian, "Find a man with a long, black mustache". Jim immediately ran to the man who had a long black mustache and pointed at him. Another Scientist instructed in the German language 'Find and show a boy with long and light hair'. Jim immediately found him and showed him. In this way, questions were being asked in multiple languages; the dog understands it and answers it in his own way.

In 1936 Jim's eyes winded. He was now not so interested in future predictions. Jim's owner, Sam Van Arsdale, also decided to keep him out of public relations. But, that year was an election year. Everyone wanted to know who would win the election. Even Sam couldn't stay out of it. He decided to ask Jim this question. Sam questioned Jim and he responded in his own way 'Roosevelt'. At the time, no one expected Roosevelt to win. They felt that this Dog was giving the wrong answer as he was getting old and was about to lose his sight. But when he died in 1937, as he had shown, Franklin Roosevelt became president again.

In the memory of Jim, a Park and a Museum have been dedicated. The park is located on the former site of his owner's hotel. Jim's grave represented by a simple headstone at Marshall Ridge Park Cemetery is one of the most visited graves on the site and it is rare to find it without flowers.

THE SUPER *Psychic*

Name – Dr. David Hoy
Birth – 21 July 1930 Evansville, Vanderburgh County, Indiana USA.
Death – 2 April 1981 at the Age of 50 Paducah, McCracken County, Kentucky, USA.

Australian author John Godwin was a crime reporter and foreign correspondent. He visited the United States of America in 1962. At that time, he met the American 'Super Psychic' Dr. David Hoy At first, he thought that David's psychic or transcendental power would be a trick or hypocrisy, and based on his long-winded experiences, he would unravel the shackles of his cunningness, but he failed.

On the contrary, being overwhelmed by his psychic powers, he stayed with him for a long time and studied him. He also wrote a book based on his long experience – '**Super – psychic: The Incredible Dr. Hoy**'. In it, he writes that "David does not fit into the framework of the psychic powers we see. He does not believe in occultism, doesn't see in the crystal balls, doesn't go into trance nor hears the voices of demons or receives the help of divine power. Yet he has tremendous, unbelievable psychic powers. He was able to find any mysterious secrets, lost things or persons, criminals and murderers, Anything about the past or future within a few seconds. **His power has been used by many people around the world.**

David Hoy was a man of extraordinary psychic powers. He kept his powers accessible to every man of the people. Anyone could contact him anytime. If a problem arose in front of him, he would answer it immediately, in which he seldom erred. No matter how many questions one had, he kept constantly answering them without getting tired. He didn't even have to think about it, as soon as the question was asked, it would be solved. Sometimes the questioner was stopped before he could finish his sentence and Hoy solves the problem".

Godwin says "When I heard about him, I wanted to meet him. When I wrote him to his home in Paducah, Kentucky, He immediately replied – 'You can come to see me anytime, anywhere.' When I went to see him, I saw that he was so well known that anyone in the city could show his home just by his name. Seeing me, Dr. Hoy gave a welcoming smile and said, "It's good that you were able to come. Giving up the idea of returning to Australia was just right. Your Mother is fine now and she has been given discharge from the hospital in Melbourne". I was shocked to hear this. During my visit to America, I did not inform anyone about my Mother's illness. She was discharged from the hospital just yesterday. She was hospitalized with a heart – attack. I congratulated on his strength and decided to spend much time with him to learn about his power.

During this period, Dr. Hoy received many letters. I used to sit with him while replying to his letters. In one such letter, a mother expressed concern about her daughter's disappearance and asked where she was and when will she come. In response, David wrote, "Mrs., your daughter is fine, she fled to New York with her friend. You will receive news from her in early May, she will come home too." The letter came from the woman in the First week of May. She said David's Prophecy came true and her daughter returned home from New York.

Once, I heard an old with anxious voice on the phone while sitting at his studio "Mr. Hoy! I lost $20. This is not a big amount but for me, it is a big amount. I really need this money right now. I can't find it anywhere in the house. Can you tell me that...?" Before he was able to complete, Dr. Hoy start describing "Oh! That's a $20 cover it is not at your home. You forgot it in a Store. Wait a minute! Let me tell you what that Store is like". After a few seconds he started saying..."The Store sells dry goods. It also sells magazines and stationery. There are two gas pumps outside the store, The Green gas pumps. The Owner of the Store is with your $20 cover. He did not steal it. You forgot it so he has kept it. He is waiting for its owner. If you go there, he will give it to you soon". The old voice replied "Mr. Hoy! You are right, this is the last store I went to this morning, it was the same store you described." He called again a couple of hours later and said he had received his $20 cover from that store!

One afternoon in December 1967, Louisville Courier Journal's staff reporter Brenda Tirey visited David Hoy's home in Evansville. She asked David, "What will be the outcome of next year's Kentucky Derby?" He said, "Horse number 4 will win." Kentucky Derby held a year later and really the horse number 4 won!

Brenda also asked David "Do you want to change the prediction you made about President Johnson at WROZ station last week. You said President Johnson would lose next year. However, at present his popularity is 10 points higher than in October and still going up. Dr Hoy replied, "It doesn't matter what the referendum says right now. I will stick to my word. Johnson will not be elected president next year". History has shown that this is exactly what happened.

Another prophecy concerning the President is note-worthy. Dr. Hoy was returning in a car from Nashville, Tennessee. The car was driven by his friend Ronald E. Decord. He turned ON the car's radio to keep himself awake at night. David was snoring in his seat, his sleep suddenly broke and he asked in a sleepy voice, "What time is it?" Ronald looked at the dashboard clock and said "It's 2 o'clock at night." David replied, "Remember this time exactly. I just saw President Johnson's plane catch fire. However, nothing happened to the President. An hour later, they heard the news on the radio that the President's jet had landed in Sydney

Airport. When its wings were running on the runway, it collided with the Gasoline truck and caught fire but it was immediately taken under control and there was no casualty.

David also announced a Plane crash at a meeting of the Michigan Metropolitan Dinner Club of Market County on January 16, 1971.

Baroga Day reporter of the OMINIG JOURNAL represented it word to word 'The next major Airline crash in the world will occur within 18 days in either Switzerland or Spain. There will be no more than two survivors, one of them will be a young boy. On January 18, a four-engine Bulgarian airplane crashed into a hill while landing in Zurich, Switzerland 35 of the 37 people travelling in it died. The only survivors were a pilot and a 12-year-old boy. Thousands of such predictions were made by David Hoy, in which he has hardly been proven wrong.

On 2 April, 1981 when David Hoy died 'The Paducah Sun' The local newspaper reported about him.

THE PADUCAH SUN NEWSPAPER ARTICLE ABOUT DR. DAVID HOY

The Paducah Sun

PADUCAH, KY.

PAGE 2—C

SUNDAY, APRIL 5, 1981

David Hoy: a remarkable man

One of the most remarkable facts about David Hoy was his almost matter-of-fact attitude to what appeared to be an uncanny gift.

He made his living by displaying the gift, an apparent ability to see and know things beyond the ability of the ordinary senses to tell him, the faculty we call extra-sensory perception.

Yet, though his profession was a kind of show business, there was no hokum or fakery in his work. He saw his gift as an ability that many people, perhaps all, have at least in latent form.

Mr. Hoy had no time for charlatans and humbuggery. So he understood skepticism about his gift. He even encouraged it.

And when some of his famous predictions failed to come true, as not uncommonly they did, he accepted the failure with a shrug. He didn't claim infallibility.

It was as if he were simply inviting other people to observe with him a remarkable ability, which pointed to some reality beyond that which is accessible to the other senses.

He did make some astounding predictions — Jackie Kennedy's marriage to Aristotle Onassis, the collapse of an Ohio River bridge, Lyndon Johnson's decision not to run for reelection. We can't explain them — and we can't explain them away.

Mr. Hoy didn't try to explain it either. He just insisted on its reality. He didn't want to be a celebrity in the usual sense. He wanted no plush apartment, no retinue of hangers-on, no persistent ballyhoo.

He wanted to live quietly and raise a family in a quiet town. That's what he came to Paducah to do, and that's what he did.

Mr. Hoy gave Paducah a spot in the national consciousness without sacrificing dignity and decorum.

His death at the age of 50 is an untimely and shocking loss to the community, and we join with many others in extending our sympathy to his exemplary family.

Renowned psychic Hoy dies at 50

Dr. David E. Hoy, a Paducah psychic whose predictions were carried in a syndicated column in 350 newspapers nationwide, died at 4:06 a.m. today at Western Baptist Hospital.

Death was attributed to a heart attack.

Hoy, 50, was a native of Evansville, Ind., and had written several books on topics relating to extra sensory perception.

His accuracy on predictions sometimes shocked him, he said in a Paducah Sun interview last week, but never wanted to frighten people about events he perceived as imminent.

"If someone asked me about their future, and I felt they were facing a serious illness or death, I wouldn't try to scare them," he said. "I would tell them they needed to see a doctor and hope that they went soon."

Hoy said he got his first taste of knowing the unknown as a child when he would tell his minister father his perceptions about congregation members.

Perhaps the prediction that he remembered the most concerned his father, the Rev. Clarence Hoy.

On the morning of March 10, 1952, Hoy suddenly turned to one of his fellow students at Bob Jones University in South Carolina and announced in a strange-sounding voice that "My father is going to die today."

His father, considered to be in good health, that day suffered a fatal heart attack at the age of 49.

Hoy wrote a weekly column for 350 suburban newspapers across the country and currently was taping "Tomorrow's News Today," a series of 90-second segments about his predictions for broadcast on cable TV networks.

He also planned to work on a possible contract with NBC on a show starring Wesley Ure about psychic phenomenon.

Survivors include his wife, Mrs. Shirley Hoy; his mother, Mrs. Margaret Hoy, Evansville; two sons, Jon Hoy, Paducah, and Van Hoy, a student at Western Kentucky

Continued On Page 10

Hoy . . .

(Continued From Page 1)

State University; a daughter, Miss Kim Hoy, Paducah; a brother, Phil Hoy, Georgia; a sister, Mrs. Margie Morris, Clarksville, Tenn., and a grandchild.

Memorial services will be scheduled later. The body will be cremated.

Roth Funeral Home is in charge of arrangements. There will be no visitation.

To know more about this fact 'Extra sensory perception' You can search :-

1) Use of Psychic in Law Enforcement 

2) How Annette Martin Helped 
   Solve a Gruesome Murder

3) Investigating 'Psychic Detectives': Four Cases 

4) The Psychic Detective Who Solved Real Crimes 

5) The Clairvoyants in America's Got Talent 

To know more about 'Extra Sensory perception' and other amazing cases you can read these Books:-

1) Edgar Cayce's ESP
2) Insight – Sylvia Browne
3) Psychic Discoveries Behind the Iron Curtain
4) ESP in Life and Lab: Tracing Hidden Channels - Louisa E.Rhine
5) True Experiences in PROPHECY - Edited By Martin Ebon
6) The Sixth Sense of Animals - Maurice Burton

+ +

Logic Four

In our body, to know anything around us we have 5 senses as follows:-

1) Skin 2) Tongue 3) Nose 4) Eyes 5) Ears.

For once let's observe where they work

1) Skin - can sense (feel) only those objects which come in touch.

2) Tongue - can sense (taste) only those objects which come in touch.

3) Nose - can sense (smell) only those objects whose smell particles come in contact.

4) Eyes - can sense (see) only those objects that don't have any non-transparent obstacles in between (even darkness is an obstacle) and are at a proper distance neither extremely near nor far away.

5) Ears - can sense (hear) only the objects whose sound vibrations come in contact.

We can conclude that all the five senses in our body **work within a limit,** Skin and tongue have a limit of touch; **They can't work beyond that;** Nose and ears have a limit of contact (of smell particles/sound vibrations); **they can't work beyond that.** Eyes have the limit of obstacles; **they can't work beyond that.**

All the five senses have a limit of distance as shown. Moreover, they do have one more limit, that is the limit of time. All five senses can only sense what is present in the current moment. They cannot sense the past or the future. For example, our eyes can only see what is presently and directly in front of us. Eyes can't even see 5 minutes past or future view. Similarly, all five senses have the limit of time, **they can't work beyond that.**

Where there is a body, there is a limit, because the body itself does exist within the limits of birth and death, **it can't work beyond that.**

Now the question is, if the body cannot work beyond its limit, how was it possible for Jim or Mr. David to know beyond the time and the distance? Isn't it surprising, a person can see or describe the scenarios related to the past or future that are absolutely absent at present, indeed, actually - completely **non-existent stuffs**. Even though, it is possible to know such things and situations; **it is a fact, a true reality that is proven by many individuals**.

For once again, I repeat the question: - If, the body cannot work beyond its limit, how was it possible for Jim or Mr. David to know beyond the time and beyond the distance? The answer is **"SOUL"**.

To know, beyond the limits of distance and time, is only possible for the Soul. Which by nature, is never been created nor ever able to be destructed. "Soul" works beyond the limits of birth and death. "Soul" has a start less - endless infinite existence of itself by nature. Similarly "Soul" itself has an ability to know everything. Everything defines: 1) every object (small or big, visible or invisible...), 2) Every place (near or far), 3) Every time (infinite past, present, and infinite future),

4) Every emotion (happy or sad, angry or calm, arrogant or humble, innocent or deceitful, selfless or selfish, each and every feelings).

Nothing is hidden from the natural all-knowing nature of the soul. And that's the only reason due to which spiders are superb builders, elephants are focused investigators, ants are fantastic architects, etc, etc, etc.....

For reading more similar article Scan the QR Code.

1) Conspicuous Social Signaling Drives Evolution Of Chameleon Color Change

2) Cuttlefish Masters Of Disguise Despite Colorblindness

3) Buzz off: Popular insect repellents pack a powerful 'one-two' punch

4) Elephantnose Fish 'See' With Their Chin

All the above animals, insects or plants were never informed, explained or trained to develop these skills, they were totally unaware. Their present brain of the present body was never programmed before to gain this proficiency. Despite this, they accurately know the unknown knowledge. The only reason responsible for such awareness, such knowledge is:- I repeat again, "The imbibed all-knowing nature of The Self, The Soul." By this, the existence of a soul is proven along with the additional fact, the 4th truth, which we can derive from this fact - "It is possible to know beyond the limits of time and distance by ESP (Extra Sensual Perception)". Some may even say it is clairvoyance, 6th sense, etc. but according to the religious terminology it is called as Vibhanggnyan and when this ability is accompanied by the surrendership to 'The Kevali', It is termed as Avadhignyan.

Want to know more about the Nature of Soul? Why can only some person have the ability of Vibhangnyan and Avadhignyan? Want to know who is this 'Kevali'? Then don't miss my upcoming book

"ORIGIN OF THE ORIGINAL".

DEATH –
THAT'S A NEW START

Long ago, there was a Kingdom. It had a weird rule. The King there was selected by a lucky draw picked by the previous King. The selected King enjoys the reign for the next 5 years. In the end, he picks the lucky draw and passes The Kingdom to the next King. Once the New King is throned, the Old King is forced to the seashore. The Old King starts crying, shouts a lot, and pleads for his rescue, but no one responds to his request. In the presence of the New King and all the citizens, the Old King is dragged to a boat by a group of soldiers and led to an Island. An Island full of wild animals, all the previous kings were dumped over here, and now their existence was just hidden within the skulls and skeletons scattered on the rocks. The Old King is thrown there alone; he has nothing with him, no family, no servants, no bed, no food, no gems, no water or anything else. The soldiers return to the kingdom leaving the King alone. And the King over there mourns aloud, as if demanding and waiting to die and also end his existence.

This was the rule of that Kingdom, Every King had to be selected – enjoy the Kingdom – select the New King and finally be thrown to die on the Scary Jungle Island.

Whenever the New King is selected he feels himself lucky till the exclusion of the Old King, as he was able to see his own future in that Old King. But, when the King returns to the palace and the days pass, the sentiments of fear disappear and he gets absorbed in the role and fun as The King and at last has the same END on The Scary Island. Many Kings passed on this way.

Once, it happened that a New King after being selected started a different routine from all the Earlier Kings. All the Earlier Kings were somewhat focused on the administration of the Kingdom and most of their time they spent having fun as much as they could.

This King had an exceptional disposition; he cared somewhat for the administration of the kingdom. But, despite having fun he focused on developing the Jungle Island, he sent troops to the jungle island, started to make a strong defense wall surrounding the forest area, built a complete township, settled business hubs, shifted many families, and finally established a kingdom over there. During the five years of his reign, he didn't have any fun but with great effort, day and night, he just worked hard to make the jungle island prosperous and finally, when the last day of his reign came, he just simply selected the New King and proceeded for his ever-lasting Kingdom 'The New Jungle Island' He didn't need to be forced anyway. As here, he worked hard to settle his whole future. The Title of The King which was going to give him a Merciful Death lent him Everlasting Joy.

It's a metaphor that gives us an understanding of the current situation of our current life according to the REALITY of the Nature. As the King was selected by a lucky draw among all the citizens to be the King, we are selected by a lucky-draw-like merit or fortune among the entire living creature to be a human. To a particular extent, the progress of spiritual development is carried ahead by default [Just due to the unconditional tolerance of sorrow (dukh)] because at those stages we didn't have any sense of understanding as we were a sensual handicap through the incarnations like various types of plants, insects, animals, birds, etc. But now, as we are a HUMAN, we are able to create a proper understanding and follow that. For now, we are King of ourselves, we can live, and behave in our own conscious manner. This life as human had made us 'The King'. **The Nature is completely aware of this situation.** It helped us till its limit, but now for the further progress, it's our own responsibility and if we fail for that effort before we leave this birth, The whole luck = the human birth becomes a waste and again, no matter how much we were successful or enjoyed a luxurious life, we are again that unfortunate one, a sensual handicap, whose complete future is just a result of a mistake, a could do but won't do impression, until, he gets the opportunity again. **Nature gives you the authority to design your future which was resisted till the date.**

We have the complete right to design our future, we have a so-called 5 years of reign that's the time until we die, and after that, it is fixed that we will have to leave willingly or unwillingly, for the jungle island that's the upcoming life, the upcoming incarnation.

Until we die, we have two options either to focus on this temporal kingdom like the present incarnation, or focus on the upcoming permanent kingdom like the infinite future. (Here I will suggest reading the chapter 'The Third Type' and all the logical parts once again). We know that to focus on the present incarnation we need Money, Family, Reputation, Business, Home, Health, Entertainment, etc., but to focus on the **next infinite future we need WHAT?**

For that we need guidance. All religions claim themselves as the guidance provider, all of them have different beliefs and ethics which they provide for the betterment of the upcoming infinite future.

The difference in religion cannot create a difference in nature. The nature has its own specific existence and law. Hence, the religion must be also of a specific, particular type. So, it's impossible to quote that there are different religions and all are perfect.

The religion to be followed must be in complete agreement of Nature and we will discuss about it in the next book

"ORIGIN OF THE ORIGINAL"

ATTACHMENT 1: REAL LIFE PHOTOS OF ALL INCIDENTS TAKEN IN THIS BOOK

THE POLLOCK TWINS

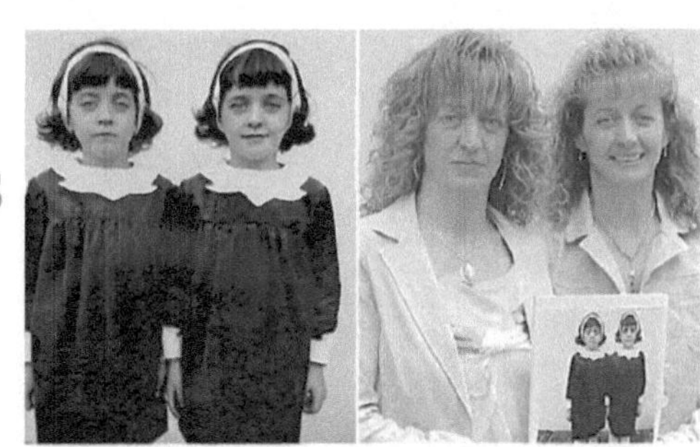

THE PERSON WHO CAUGHT HIS MURDERER (TITU SINGH)

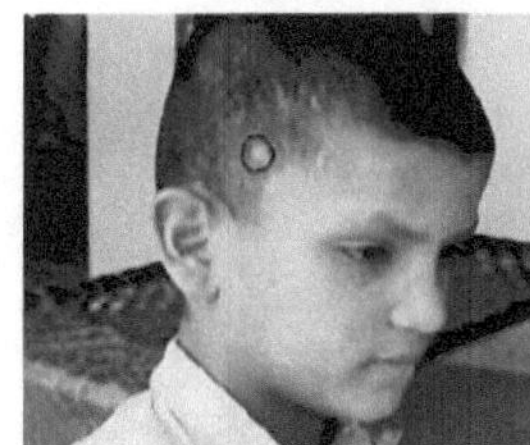

PAST LIFE BULLET MARK   SURESH RADIOS SHOP IN AGRA   SURESH WIFE (UMA VERMA)

CHAIR OF DEATH

BUSBY CHAIR

THE DEAD STILL ON DUTY
(CAPTAIN HARBHAJAN SINGH)

SEARCH FOR GRACE

SEARCH FOR GRACE
MOVIE POSTER

SEARCH FOR GRACE
BOOK

JIM 'THE WONDER DOG'

JIM REAL PHOTO

JIM PARK

JIM GRAVE STONE

JIM THE WONDER DOG MUSEUM

THE SUPER PSYCHIC

DR. DAVID HOY

THE SUPER-PSYCHIC BOOK

ATTACHMENT 2:
ALL REFERENCE BOOKS PHOTO SUGGESTED IN THIS BOOK

RECOLLECTION OF PAST LIFE MEMORIES

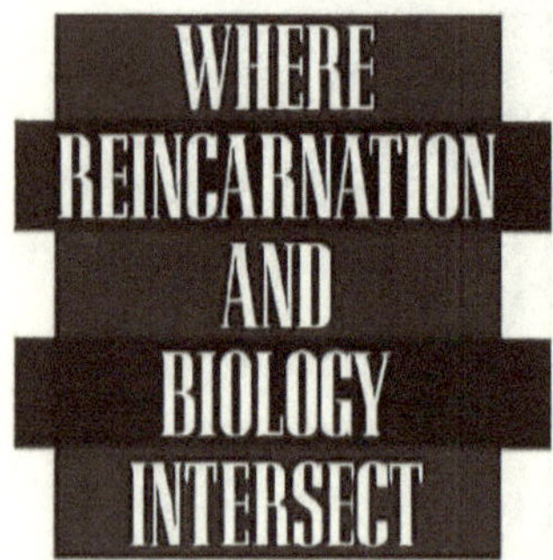

WHERE
REINCARNATION AND
BIOLOGY INTERSECT
- IAN STEVENSON, M.D.

CHILDREN'S PAST
LIVES
- CAROL BOWMAN

LIFETIMES – TRUE
ACCOUNTS OF
REINCARNATION
– FREDERICK LENZ

LIFE BEFORE BIRTH
– PETER AND MARY
HARRISON

YOU WILL LIVE AGAIN
– BRAD STEIGER

EXISTENCE OF GHOST

HAUNTED ROYAL HOMES
- JOAN FORMAN

30 YEARS AMONG THE DEAD
- CARL WICKLAND M.D.

THE GHOST WHISPERER
- KATIE COUTTS

GHOST WATCH
- COLIN GARDNER

UNDERSTANDING GHOSTS
- VICTORIA BRANDEN,
VICTOR GOLLANCZ

GHOST SIGHTINGS
- COLLIN WILSON

PAST LIFE REGRESSION THERAPY

THE SEARCH FOR BRIDE
MURFY
– MOREY BERNSTEIN

PAST LIVES, FUTURE
LIVES
– DR. BRUCE GOLDBERG

LIFE BEFORE LIFE
– HELEN WAMBACH

MANY LIVES, MANY
MASTERS
– DR. BRIAN WEISS

JOURNEY OF SOULS
– MICHAEL NEWTON PHD.

EXTRA SENSORY PRECEPTION

EDGAR CAYCE'S ESP
- KEVIN J. TODESCHI

INSIGHT
– SYLVIA BROWNE

ESP IN LIFE AND LAB:
TRACING HIDDEN
CHANNELS
- LOUISA E.RHINE

PSYCHIC DISCOVERIES
BEHIND THE IRON
CURTAIN
- SHEILA OSTRANDER,
LYNN SCHROEDER,
IVAN T. SANDERSON

TRUE EXPERIENCES IN
PROPHECY
- EDITED BY MARTIN
EBON

THE SIXTH SENSE OF
ANIMALS
- MAURICE BURTON